Real Estate

Agents EXposed

*How to Hire the Right Agent and
Kick the Others to the Curb*

David Smithers

Real Estate Agents Exposed: How to Hire the Right Agent and Kick the Others to the Curb
Copyright ©2020 David Smithers

ISBN: 9798676567057

For Discussion and Updates, Visit Us at:
www.AgentsExposed.com

TABLE OF CONTENTS

INTRODUCTION

If you have ever bought or sold a home, chances are good that one or more real estate agents were involved in the process. [i]In a recent year, both 89% of Sellers and 89% of Buyers were assisted by a real estate agent in their real estate transaction. 11% of homes were sold FSBO (For Sale by Owner).

Some residential real estate agents are great, some are downright awful, and then there are a whole slew of them that are mediocre. I should know, because until recently, I was a real estate agent myself, and I know what is going on inside the real estate industry due to my years of assisting others in buying and selling their homes.

I have seen many agents who had no business being in the business. You would be shocked to learn how many can barely use a calculator, let alone engage in complex negotiations. Being a real estate agent is one of the few occupations where you can go from getting a license to declaring yourself a "Top Agent" in a matter of weeks, and no one seems to question it.

Since the real estate agent is mostly responsible for his or her own business, the lack of professionalism by many agents is astounding. The number of missed appointments, unanswered calls and texts, and downright sloppiness with paperwork has become the norm for many agents. The biggest complaint agents make about each other has to do with the lack of communication in the middle of a deal.

And with many agents working part-time (although most won't tell you that), where do you think their focus is going to be? Do you think they are going to be available when you need them the most? Many of these agents have other full or part-time jobs that demand specific days and hours and are only able to do real estate in their free time. How effective do you think they're going to be if they've put in 40 hours that week at another job? In today's market with multiple offers being made on many of the most desirable homes, and strict deadlines, you need someone who is not only sharp, but available.

We also know that many real estate agents never sell one house in an average year, and many only sell one or two. Agents like that might have ten years of experience as far as the calendar is concerned, but extraordinarily little actual hands-on experience in real estate transactions. For instance, in my market we had approximately 4,000 agents, but on average we only had 2,000 homes on the market. And many of the agents who did have listings had anywhere from a few, to 20 or more. That tells you that many of them had none.

Longevity is another issue. Almost every survey of real estate agents agrees that 4 out of 5 agents will drop out within two years of being in the business. Don't you want someone you know is going to be there to see your particular transaction all the way through?

My purpose in writing this book is not to steer you away from real estate agents (although in some cases they are not necessary), but to steer you away from the mediocre to bad agents and show you how to find a good one. And if your circumstances warrant it, to encourage you to try selling your home on your own and saving a whole lot of money.

Before we jump into it, let me give one explanatory note concerning the terms "Real Estate Agent" and "Realtor®." A Real Estate agent is anyone who is licensed to sell real estate. [ii]A Realtor® is a licensed real estate agent who is also a member of the National Association of Realtors® (NAR). So, you can be a real estate agent without being a Realtor®, but you cannot be a Realtor® without being a real estate agent. To make things simple, I will refer to everyone licensed to sell real estate as Real Estate Agents in this book.

Where social media conversations are included, I have not included names, and in some cases, have changed the content just enough that the participants cannot be recognized.

IMPORTANT NOTE: You need to be aware that I am not an attorney and I am not offering legal advice in any way, shape, or form. If you have legal questions, please consult an attorney that specializes in real estate issues.

1. HOW HARD IS IT TO GET A REAL ESTATE LICENSE?

For a moment let's pretend that you have decided to enter into an industry where you will be responsible for making sure your client's most valuable possession, worth anywhere from tens of thousands to multiple millions of dollars, is transferred from their ownership to a prospective buyer, with everything going smoothly. You will need to make sure that you have priced this item correctly, in an ever fluctuating market where the price for a very similar item can vary widely based on location, quality of materials, upgrades, and many other factors. You also will need to carefully evaluate when the best time is to sell, how to market most effectively, and what steps you will take to ensure the potential buyer is qualified to make the purchase and will be able to come up with the necessary financing. In addition, you will need to know how to best communicate all of the above to your client to help them to both understand and buy into your pricing strategy, as well as instruct them how they can best cooperate in making this process work as easily as possible. Of course, we are talking here about listing and selling someone's home.

Considering all the above, and much more that I've left out, how much education do you think is necessary prior to being able to sit for a real estate license exam? Here in my area, most car dealerships require their salespeople to at least have an associate degree before they'll let them sell cars. In fact, I've noticed that many, if not most, sales positions require some type of college-level training, even though many of these positions do not require anywhere close to the amount of knowledge concerning finance, construction, and marketing that is needed by the average real estate agent.

The educational requirements vary State by State, but the vast majority require that a prospective real estate agent must meet the minimum requirements of being 18-years-old, have a high school diploma or equivalent (GED), and take pre-licensing courses. The average number of hours for pre-licensing courses is about 60, though some States require less and some substantially more. And you need to understand that these are clock hours, not semester hours. If you were to take a three-hour college course, that means you attend that class three hours per week for an entire semester (or trimester, etc...). So, in a normal 16-week semester, you've spent 48 clock hours in a three-hour course, plus completed assignments, taken tests, and written papers. To get an associate degree, most schools require 60 semester hours to graduate. Which translates to 960 clock hours of class time alone. In pre-licensing for real estate, 60 hours is 60 literal hours on the clock.

So with a high school diploma or GED, and a minimum number of clock hours (usually about a week to week and a half worth of classes), you have completed your educational requirements to sit for the real estate agent exam. And what have you learned in those classes? Have you learned how to accurately price a home? How to market? How to be a people person? No, because the training has nothing to do with sales. The training is all about legalities, measurements, ordinances, and the like. Not that those things aren't important, but they have very little, if anything, to do with preparing you to be responsible for someone's $500,000 investment.

To make matters worse, in most States the class is not a typical class where you have homework, tests, and are expected to regurgitate the material for the instructor. They are more like seminars where you simply go and listen. In other words, plant your rear end on a seat for the required number of hours, and you are ready to take the exam!

The exam itself is not overly difficult if you have taken the time to study, but it is not unusual for it to take two or three attempts to pass. This is mainly due to the many questions dealing with topics most real estate agents will never face in their careers, including questions about how to divide acreage into lots, topographical issues, and more.

Once the exam is passed it is time to move onto placing your license with a broker. Which, as we will see, isn't very difficult either.

2. BROKERS CANNOT AFFORD TO BE CHOOSY

Once a person passes their license exam it is time to align themselves with a broker. The great thing about this for the newly minted agent is, almost every broker wants you to sign up with them. There are an exceedingly small number of brokerages that are selective and will only take on established agents with a good track record, but those are few and far between.

There are literally thousands of brokerages out there, with several of them being exceptionally large outfits. Some are franchises and some are individually owned. Some of the bigger names out there are Keller Williams, eXp, ReMax, Coldwell Banker, Century 21, United, ERA, Berkshire

Hathaway, and many, many more. Outnumbering the bigger brokerages by total number of agents in many areas are small companies that you might have never heard of. Many of these could only have one agent/broker, or might have dozens.

The name of the game with most brokerages is volume, both in number of agents and number of transactions. If you are an agent, you need someone with a broker's license to put your license under. But guess what? The broker needs you as well. While some brokerages, like eXp, have done away with the traditional office environment, most still have them. Who do you think is going to pay the lease for office space, copiers, computers, the salaries of management, and the many other expenses the broker has to pay out each month? The agent is.

Most brokerages charge some type of an office, or desk fee. The average is around $75 per month, although some charge more and some less. Some charge in addition to the office fee for copies, desk space, website, and other practical needs. Others include those expenses, but you usually will pay a higher split (we'll get to that in a moment).

Let's say that the monthly fee is $75.00. If that broker has 100 agents, they are bringing in $7,500 each month in office fees alone. If they have 200 agents, they are bringing in $15,000 per month, and so on.

In addition to that, each agent signs an agreement with the broker that specifies, among other things, what their commission split is going to be. There is a wide variety of splits and ways of doing this, but at many companies an agent starts out with a lower split, and then with more sales, can receive a more favorable split.

A split is just what it sounds like – the agent and the broker are going to split the commission that was brought in on a sale. Let's say that an agent listed and sold a house for $500,000 and charged a 6% commission. That means that $30,000 (6%) is going to be taken out of the Seller's proceeds when they sell their house. Usually that commission is split evenly between the Seller's brokerage and the Buyer's brokerage, which is the most common scenario. $15,000 will go to the Seller's brokerage, and $15,000 will go to the Buyer's brokerage. Each agent is going to hand that $15,000 check to his or her broker and the broker is going to take out their split, and then write out a new check (or direct deposit) for the remaining amount to the agent. If the split is 50/50, both the broker and the agent will walk away with $7,500. Usually the splits these days are much more favorable to the agent, like 70/30, 80/20, or sometimes even 100% to the agent, with a fee per transaction taken out by the broker.

All the explanation above leads me to this – the more transactions the agent makes, the more the broker earns. This should give the broker the motivation to make sure and train their agents to be the best salespeople they can possibly be, even though, unfortunately, this is usually not the case. Many brokers are completely satisfied earning a monthly office fee that they know they are going to get whether the agent makes any sales or not. When they do make a sale, which many never do, it is icing on the cake.

The key to this is getting warm bodies into the brokerage. The more agents you can get in your office, the more money you are going to make for the brokerage. One of the main jobs of a real estate broker or manager, is recruiting. Get on **www.indeed.com** or some other job recruiting website and search for "real estate agent." You'll be shocked at all the ads from local brokerages. And they put these ads up constantly because most brokerages are a revolving door. If you do not keep bringing new people in every month, you soon will not have any agents to get your fees from. Many times I have seen agents brought on board that everyone, including the broker most of all, knew had absolutely no chance of making it in real estate. It happens all the time in almost every brokerage.

You can see why most brokers can't afford to be choosy. To bring in agents, they have to offer nice facilities, training, office staff, agent websites and more, because they are competing against every other brokerage in the area. But to pay for all of those things agents want and need, they have to spend a lot of money. So, to cover their expenses, and still make a sizeable profit, they need to keep adding more and more newly licensed agents.

This brings me to this sad truth – there are a lot of agents out there who should not be selling real estate. I am not exaggerating when I say that there are licensed agents who can barely do basic addition and subtraction, let alone understand some of the complexities of today's mortgage industry. I have sat in on many meetings with the people

I'm describing, as well as read many of their posts in private real estate social media forums, and can tell you without hesitation, you really need to be careful when you hire an agent to help you sell or buy a house.

In addition to that, there are many agents who simply do not have personalities or make lifestyle choices that are conducive to selling real estate. Obviously, there is not a "one-type-fits-all" sales personality, as there are many different types of people and some fit better with one agent than another. But when you have agents with the personality of a loaf of bread, or who have bad hygiene, or drink a lot (on the job), or cannot complete a sentence without dropping the "F Bomb," they're probably not going to be in real estate long term.

I'm not saying this to be mean, and I'm not saying these people are stupid – I am saying they do not have a nose for real estate in particular and you should be aware that there are a lot of them out there. Do you really want to trust your biggest investment to a person who does not know what they are doing and could cost you thousands of dollars? And guess what? The agents I'm warning you about have websites, literature, and presentation material that looks just as nice and slick as the agents who have their acts together. But don't worry, I am going to tell you how to tell the good agents from the bad in the chapter on Interviewing Agents.

3. DESIGNATIONS AND CERTIFICATIONS

In many professions it is not uncommon to put the initials of your relevant credentials next to your name on business cards and other literature. For instance: John Doe, Ph.D. or Jane Doe, M.B.A. The funny thing is, you see something remarkably similar with real estate agents, but normally they are not listing their degrees, but different designations and/or certifications they have earned.

> [iii]"We can make as much money as doctors and lawyers, and they spend tens of thousands of dollars on their degrees," Rae Wayne, a Realtor® with the Bizzy Blondes team in Los Angeles.

Here are some of the [iv]designations and certifications that are presently accepted by the National Association of Realtors®.

Designations:

ABR® - Accredited Buyer's Representative
ALC   - Accredited Land Consultant
CCIM - Certified Commercial Investment Member
CIPS   - Certified International Property Specialist
CPM®- Certified Property Manager
CRB   - Certified Real Estate Brokerage Manager
CRS   - Certified Residential Specialist
CRE® - Counselor of Real Estate
GAA   - General Accredited Appraiser
GRI   - Graduate, REALTOR® Institute
PMN   - Performance Management Network
RCE   - REALTOR®, Association Certified Executive
RAA   - Residential Accredited Appraiser
SRS   - Seller Representative Specialist
SIOR - Society of Industrial and Office REALTORS®
SRES® - Senior Real Estate Specialist

Certifications:

AHWD- At Home With Diversity
BPOR - Broker Price Opinion Resource
C-RETS- Certified Real Estate Team Specialist
e-PRO®
MRP   - Military Relocation Professional
PSA   - Pricing Strategy Advisor
RENE - Real Estate Negotiation Expert
RSPS - Resort & Second Home Property Specialist
SFR® - Short Sales & Foreclosure Resource

Let me say right off the bat that the National Association of Realtors® DOES NOT claim that these are college degrees or that the courses are at the college level. They give accurate descriptions of each of these Designations and Certifications on their website at:

https://www.nar.realtor/education/designations-and-certifications

The problem is that many real estate agents strongly imply that they have earned something similar to a college degree when they list what designations and certifications they have received. I have been personally coached to include my designations and certifications in listing presentations and to "puff" them up to sound like I have spent many grueling hours studying to earn them. Nothing could be further from the truth.

While there are designations, like the CRS and GRI, that take quite a bit of time and effort to earn, most are accomplished by paying a fee (sometimes recurring) and attending a class. Both designations I have earned consisted entirely of listening to lectures read off of a

Power Point presentation for two days by an instructor. That was it.

But surely, there was a test to make sure you had retained all that knowledge? Well, yes, there was a test in both cases. And in both cases the teacher went over the answers to each question with the entire class while we were taking the test to make sure we all got the answers correct. In other words, we were given the answers. You could have easily slept through the entire two days of lectures and you still would have walked out with the designation. Immediately after I "earned" my first designation the real estate agent next to me said, "I didn't learn anything but at least I can put some letters after my name."

Here's a question for you. Would you consider someone who spent a couple of days sitting through classes an expert on their subject? Many agents promote themselves as exactly that.

> v"Yes, designations are worth it, but you have to leverage it once you receive it. If you work hard to receive a particular designation but then fail to market the fact that you are now an

endorsed expert in a particular real estate niche, then your designation won't get you very far."

While others might have had a different experience, I can assure you that after a couple of days watching slide presentations and listening to someone drone on and on as they read their notes to the class, I was certainly not an expert on the subject. At best, I was introduced to the subject, which equipped me to realize how little I knew and made me aware that I needed much more training in these particular areas.

"[vi]My advice to new agents is to always get some kind of designation ASAP because people quit asking how long you have been in business once you get some alphabet soup after your name."

There are other companies and organizations offering designations and certifications that have no affiliation with, and are not recognized by, the National Association of Realtors®. While these might or might not hold value, it is hard to say without examining each individual program.

[vii]One interesting certification is offered by Mutual of Omaha Mortgage where a real estate agent can be "[viii]certified by Sgt. David Smith" after attending a one day class and passing a test that you are given all the answers to by the instructor (sound familiar?). Each participant receives a certificate, as well as a commemorative coin. The certificate reads as follows:

> *"Certificate of Proficiency – (Agent's Name) You are hereby formally awarded this certificate of proficiency, in appreciation of your meritorious efforts, in service to the men and women of the Armed Forces of the United States of America; for demonstrating superior knowledge and clear passion for serving others, you will from this moment forward, be recognized by theVALoan.org as a VETERAN AND ACTIVE DUTY ADVOCATING REAL ESTATE PROFESSIONAL."*

Wow! Sounds impressive doesn't it? I cannot tell you how many social media posts I have seen from real estate agents who have attended one of these seminars who now proudly and boldly declare themselves to be experts in the VA loan program. They even post pictures of themselves holding the commemorative coin and certificate as if they've really done a lot to earn them. Each agent also receives a personalized website promoting their expertise.

The following social media post is representative:

> "[ix]I am a certified VA loan specialist. Maybe the most important designation I've ever earned in Real Estate. Are you a Veteran? Let me help guide you in your next home purchase."

It is not that there is anything wrong with real estate certifications and designations. Some of them might be quite helpful, especially those that are more than a one- or two-day seminar. The problem is with those who misrepresent and exaggerate what it is they have actually accomplished. When you see that a real estate agent has included initials after their name, indicating further education, feel free to ask him or her how they earned those letters. Hopefully, they'll be honest with you.

4. YOU HAVE NEVER SEEN BIGGER EGOS

At the beginning of this chapter it is necessary to say that there are many, many wonderful people who are involved in real estate. You might not get that impression from some of what you've read so far, but it is true. I cannot tell you how many agents are truly helpful, pleasant, and go out of their way to meet the needs of their clients, as well as do their best to help out other real estate agents. The nice ones far outweigh the ones who aren't so nice. It is not unusual to have an agent give up part of their commission to make sure someone is able to get into their dream home. Other seasoned agents will often take a new agent under their wing and show them the ropes, even though there is no financial advantage to them in doing so. So, when I talk about agents with huge egos, realize that many of them are not like that at all. The problem is, while they might not be in the majority, there are many with egos the size of Texas.

Some real estate agents introduce themselves as, "John Doe, Top Agent in Anytown, USA." Others go out of their way to make sure everyone knows they are a "Mega Agent." None of these terms are defined, and even agents with very little experience will use them. A well-known real estate trainer actually advises new agents to purchase different sets of business cards with different titles such as, "Listing Specialist" or "Buyer's Specialist," as soon as they get their license, and use them according to their need at the moment. If someone tells you they are a "specialist" in any category, ask them what they have done to earn that designation.

The agents with the biggest egos love to tell all the other agents, whom they consider to be peons, how great they are. Sometimes in negotiations it is not unusual for one of these self-indulgent types to say something like, "Well, I'm a Top Agent, and I know what I'm talking about." In other words, "You need to back off, because I am the greatest thing to ever happen to the real estate world." Sometimes they like to scream at other agents over the phone and demand their way. What is really hilarious is that in most markets, any real estate agent is able to look up the sales figures for every other agent in their association and can tell if they really are a "Top Agent" or not. You'd be surprised how many "Top Agents" have barely made any sales. Of course, even if they really are successful, that is no excuse for such rude behavior. Another common tactic is for them to let you know they've been in the business for a long time. Two of the worst agents I ever dealt with both had their broker's license and had been in the real estate business for decades. Both were incredibly horrible to work with and had no idea what they were doing.

Agents love to give themselves awards. While it is not unusual in sales for awards to be given, real estate agents just cannot get enough of them. Most local real estate associations offer awards for those who are at the top in different sales categories. Both Franchise and Independent Brokers offer awards for every category imaginable based on everything from sales to community service. Some have intriguing names like "Platinum," "Diamond," or "Ambassador," to make them sound like you've really made it. Please don't misunderstand me, most agents have really worked hard to reach these levels, it is just a bit egotistical to have to get an award every time you make an accomplishment. In most industries, you are not recognized every single time you reach a new milestone. One of the most common awards is being allowed entrance into the "Million Dollar Club." Most people on the outside think that means you made $1,000,000 in a year from real estate sales. What it actually means is that you sold $1,000,000 worth of real estate. If the average home sells for $200,000 in your market, that means the agent made at least five sales. Now that isn't a bad thing, but it hardly qualifies for being at the top of the heap.

If you'd like to see some egos on display for yourself, sign up for some real estate agent Facebook groups:

Lab Coat Agents
https://www.facebook.com/groups/labcoatagents/

Zero to Diamond Real Estate Agents
https://www.facebook.com/groups/DiamondAgents/

Real Estate Rockstars
https://www.facebook.com/groups/rockstar.agents/

There are many more that you can find with a simple search, but these should give you a pretty good glimpse into the ugly world of agent egos. You will find some of the most pretentious posts imaginable. Ones like:

> *What kind of car do you drive? I've had my Audi 8 for a year now, and really need to upgrade.*

> *I've had so many sales this year that I'm actually hoping the market slows down. I don't get these crap agents who say they can't get any listings. People are literally begging me to list their homes.*

> *What do you give your clients for Closing Gifts? I usually commission a painting done of their new home and give them a year's subscription for their favorite wine, then pay their first years HOA fees. I've been thinking about doing something different. Any rad ideas?*

If you think I'm exaggerating, just check out some of the groups I've posted above. You will be astounded and dismayed at the amount of ego on display.

While it is not unusual for people to be proud of the job they do and maybe even brag about it on limited occasions, many real estate agents do this every single day, especially on social media. It gets quite nauseating for those who have to see these posts every day. Since I am friends with hundreds of real estate agents on Facebook, I see many of these every day. What I am referring to are posts like the following:

Just out and about doing my favorite thing! Loving on my clients! I would do this job even if I didn't get paid! LUV!!!!

It's Christmas Eve and guess where I'm at? Showing houses and having a blast! The fun never ends when you're making people's dreams come true!

Wassup? I'll tell you what – 3 Closings today and more to come tomorrow! You never get a break when you're a Top Agent, but I live for this stuff!

Guess who sold the most houses in July? You got it right, Me! I am so humbled right now by all of my success.

If you think the posts above are inflated or hyped in any way then you are not friends with any real estate agents. I could look at today's posts alone and easily multiply what I've shared ten-fold.

Then there are the many testimonials. While testimonials can be a great source of information for people looking for an agent, the way some agents use them is a bit over-the-top. What most people don't realize is that there are websites you can subscribe to that will help real estate agents generate testimonials from their clients. I am not claiming the testimonials are not real, just that they have a way of badgering people until they give one. Some of the sites providing these services are:

https://www.realsatisfied.com/
https://www.ratemyagent.com/

Once the testimonial is received, the agents will immediately start posting them to social media. That is, they will if it is a positive testimonial. The negative ones seem to go by the wayside. Usually the agent will say something along the lines of, "I just loved working with the John Doe family. They were the best clients ever. Are you looking to buy or sell?" There is absolutely nothing wrong with testimonials, but the way they are sometimes used shows the type of ego the agent has.

Did you know that some real estate agents have their own magazines where they can give you even more information about how great they are? They are available to any agent willing to pay for them, and many of them are more than willing. The funny thing is these magazines come from a paid service. The agent gives out these magazines to potential, current, and former clients to make it look like they are super successful. If you didn't know better (and they don't want you to know better) you'd think the real estate agent was so incredibly successful that he or she had their own real estate publishing business. But guess what? Anyone can purchase these magazines, and the publisher will gladly personalize them for you with your picture and contact information. The funny thing is, if you know more than one real estate agent that subscribes to these types of services, you will see the exact same articles and information, but personalized to make it look like the agent did this themselves. Here is a link to one of the services available.

https://remindermedia.com/real-estate-agents/

This chapter would not be complete without mentioning the personal photos that many agents use, especially those who have been around awhile. You might have thought glamour shots were a thing of the past, but you would be wrong. There is nothing more shocking than meeting an agent for the first time who is well into their 60s, but their picture is from when they were 25-years-old. This is very common in the real estate industry. And even when the picture is accurate from an age-based perspective, the touch up work on them is amazing – no wrinkles, no spots, just beauty. I've seen recent pictures of agents I know well that were so touched up that I would not have known it was them if I hadn't seen it beside their name on their business card and website!

5. HOW MUCH DO YOU CHARGE?

Most real estate agents/brokers charge a commission to those selling their home, but most buyers do not have to pay their agent anything. In the majority of markets, the Seller pays the entire commission, although there are exceptions to this in some areas. For our purposes, we will deal with the most common practice, where the Seller pays the entire amount. There are brokers who charge a flat fee, but that is not the most common way of doing business.

A commission is a percentage of the sales price. So, if a 6% commission is agreed to, the Seller will pay the real estate broker $6,000 on a $100,000 sale, leaving them with $94,000 before other expenses are paid. Look at the simple chart below to see how this works out depending on sales price, again, using 6% as our commission percentage.

Sales Price:	6% Commission:	Remainder:
$100,000	$6,000	$94,000
$200,000	$12,000	$188,000
$300,000	$18,000	$298,200
$400,000	$24,000	$376,000
$500,000	$30,000	$470,000
$600,000	$36,000	$564,000
$700,000	$42,000	$648,000
$800,000	$48,000	$752,000
$900,000	$54,000	$846,000
$1,000,000	$60,000	$940,000

Do you think it will cost the real estate agent/broker 10 times more money to sell a $1,000,000 house than a $100,000 house? The answer is a resounding NO! Depending on the situation, they might have to spend more money on advertising to get the $1,000,000 house in front of the right buyer, along with some other expenses, but there is no way it is costing them anywhere close to ten times as much.

So why does the Seller have to pay 10 times as much? Because real estate brokers through the years have done a great job convincing the public that it will take a much larger investment of their time and resources to market the more expensive house. Again, it might cost them a little bit more, but nowhere close to the amount necessary to justify such a huge increase from a less expensive house. Before the age of the internet the argument would have been a little more convincing, but the truth is, almost every house receives the same marketing. They might pay extra for signage, and advertising in magazines an executive might read, but other than that, it is pretty much the same. I am sure that many agents will disagree with what I'm saying here because it cuts into their livelihood, but it is the truth.

Let me put this as bluntly as possible – unless there are some very extreme circumstances surrounding a particular residential property making it very difficult to sell, there is no way any real estate agent is worth paying $60,000 to sell your house. But guess what? It goes on every day, all around the Country. I am not saying real estate agents shouldn't be paid, or that they shouldn't be paid well, but in my opinion, these amounts become exorbitant the higher we go up in price range.

Did you know that the commission percentage is not a set amount and is negotiable? While there are some agents and brokerages that will not lower their commission rate, the vast majority of them will when pressed to do so. While they want to get as much money as they can, it is hard to walk away from potentially tens of thousands of dollars in commission when they know another qualified agent will take the deal if they won't.

As you'll see when we get to the chapter on interviewing an agent, there are a lot of issues just as, if not more important than, commission percentage, but this is a big one. As you can see, we are talking about thousands if not tens of thousands of dollars here, so it is well worth your time to negotiate in this area.

How do you go about it? Simply ask them. Say, *what commission percentage do you usually charge?* This amount will vary by brokerage and by area of the Country. While it is against the Law for brokerages to get together and decide on a certain percentage they all will charge, it is not uncommon to find that most brokerages in a given area do charge a similar amount. For instance, in the area I worked, almost every broker I'm aware of charged 6%, but they were not allowed to discuss that amount with other brokers or agents in terms of making a set amount binding on everybody. If brokerages did get together and agree to a set amount, they could be in violation of Antitrust Law. If interested, you can read more about that at the following link:

https://www.nar.realtor/antitrust#section-171122

Before I go into objections your real estate agent might have to lowering the commission, please understand that 6% is not a set amount in all areas of the Country, nor does every broker in a given area charge the same amount. You will find that most of the larger brokerages do charge the same amount but will find a lot of different scenarios with boutique brokerages. I personally know of agents who work for brokers who insist on 6%, but the agent actually charges 7% or more so they can put more money in their own pocket. When I first started in real estate 7% was common. On the other hand, in some of the more rural areas around where I have worked, it is not uncommon for brokers to charge 5.5% or 5%. Some will even go lower than that. Let's look at the same sales but reduce the commission rate to 5% to see how much money you can save.

Sales Price:	5% Commission:	Savings:
$100,000	$5,000	$1,000
$200,000	$10,000	$2,000
$300,000	$15,000	$3,000
$400,000	$20,000	$4,000
$500,000	$25,000	$5,000
$600,000	$30,000	$7,000
$700,000	$35,000	$7,000
$800,000	$40,000	$8,000
$900,000	$45,000	$9,000
$1,000,000	$50,000	$10,000

Big savings, right? But what if we went even lower? Once you hit the $500,000 range there is no reason why the commission couldn't be lowered to closer to 4%, and once you hit $1,000,000, 3% sounds like a much more reasonable number.

There is a point where it is not going to be worth the agent's time and effort, but these sound like reasonable numbers to me. Another way of doing this would be for a brokerage to cap the commission at a certain amount. For instance, any home sold for $500,000 or more will be charged a flat fee of $20,000.

Here is where the rubber hits the road. Let's say you ask the real estate agent what their commission rate is, and they answer, "6%." You then say, "I am not willing to pay that much, how much would you be able to reduce that amount?" Now you might get an agent who says, "I am willing to go down 1% to 5% total commission, but I can't go any lower than that." But most likely you are going to get one of several possible objections to them lowering their commission at all. Most agents are trained to instantly object to lowering their commission. In fact, many of them take it personally and can get quite upset about it. Here are some of the more common objections, and some potential responses:

Common Objections to Lowering Commission:

Agent: "I'm not allowed to discuss lowering commission. It is against the Antitrust Laws."

Homeowner: "Actually, it is not. Antitrust applies to price fixing with another brokerage. I'm not asking you to do that."

Agent: "My broker will not allow me to lower the commission."

Homeowner: "I'm sorry to hear that. I will be interviewing other real estate agents more in line with what I'm willing to pay."

Agent: "If I were to lower the commission, what would that say about my negotiating skills? Don't you want a good negotiator working for you?"

Homeowner: "As a matter of fact I do. But you're not negotiating, just stating an amount and sticking with it."

Agent: "It is going to cost me a lot of money to market this property. I am barely going to make any money as is."

Homeowner: "Please show me a line item of each expense and how much each is going to cost to see if I'm being unreasonable here."

Agent: "I'm sure you are more concerned with what you are netting from the sale, not my salary. My average sale is 98% of the listing price, so you will net more on the sale than with another agent."

Homeowner: "That is great, but if you charge less commission, and then sell the home for 98% of the listing price, I'll net even more."

Agent: "I am in the Top 10% of real estate agents in this County. I am worth more."

Homeowner: "I am willing to take a chance that another Top Agent will list for less if you are not willing or able to."

Agent: "The commission I'm charging includes all the frills. What would you like me to cut if I reduce my commission?"

Homeowner: "I am expecting the full package of services at the reduced commission. If you are not able to do that, that is fine. I will be interviewing more agents."

I could go on and on, but these are real life examples of the way real estate agents are trained to get around your request for a reduced commission. My advice? Be polite, but don't back down. There are plenty of great agents who will list your home for less and do a fantastic job. And in these days when almost every industry offers coupons, rebates, or other financial incentives, why shouldn't real estate agents be willing to do the same?

All that being said, there is a real limit as to how far a real estate agent can go down on commission. Let me take a moment to explain how a commission is split up between agents and brokers.

When a real estate agent enters a new listing into the Multiple Listing Service (MLS), they have to enter a percentage that the Listing office will receive and a percentage that the Selling (Buying) office will receive. While there are times when the same agent both lists and sells your home, most often that is not the case. In many areas of the Country, it is common for the brokerages to evenly split the difference. On a 6% commission, 3% goes to the Listing office, and 3% goes to the Selling office. This is not set in stone, and I have seen the Listing office take 3.5% and offer the Selling office 2.5%, but that is generally frowned upon by many agents. Each brokerage has an arrangement with their agents as to how they will split the amount that comes to the brokerage. For instance, if an agent is on a 70/30 split, 70% goes to the agent, and 30% goes to the brokerage. To make things simple using the above example, if the commission check is $10,000, the agent will get $7,000, and the brokerage will get $3,000.

Out of these funds the broker has to pay all of their expenses – rent, staff salaries, utilities, brochures, insurance, etc… The agent has to pay dues, vehicle expenses, taxes, etc… In some cases, the broker pays for all the advertising, while in others the agent pays for advertising, or splits the cost. There are many other expenses than I have listed here. When you see the commission check as a Seller or Buyer, you see the total and it looks like a lot of money. When the agent or broker looks at that same check, in their mind they are subtracting all the cost of doing business from the total. There is a point of diminishing returns for the agent and broker. If you want them to sell your $200,000 house for 1%, there is no way they can do it, as they would lose money on the deal. In this book we are talking about being reasonable and expecting the agent and broker to be well paid for their hard work. We just don't want to overpay them.

Above I told you that the agent will enter the amount they are willing to pay the other brokerage out of the commission. If a Seller is only paying 4% commission, for example, the listing agent is most likely going to offer only 2% commission to the selling agent. That amount they are willing to pay is listed in the MLS (Multiple Listing

Service) where every other agent can see it. And while most agents won't admit to it, when they are looking for houses for their buyer, and they see they are only going to get 2% while other houses in the same price range are paying more, they are less likely to encourage their clients to go look at that house. So, you need to be careful how low you go. When you get up into the higher price ranges, it is not as big of a deal, because as we've seen previously, they are still going to get a big paycheck even with a lower percentage.

If you are using the same agent to both sell your home and help you to buy another one, many will be willing to give you a break on commission. For instance, you might say, "Since I am using you to both sell and buy a home, and you will get a commission on both sides of the deal, I'd like you to drop your commission by 1%." You could also ask them to do the same thing if they are the listing agent and they also represent the buyer (this is called dual agency and might or might not be legal in your State. More on that later.).

One last consideration under this section concerns Flat Fee Brokerages. While not as common, they are in most markets. A Flat Fee Brokerage charges a set amount, rather than a percentage. For instance, they might advertise that they will sell any house for $1,500. Or they might base the flat fee on the price of the house. One caution when dealing with Flat Fee Brokerages – find out exactly what they are offering you for that fee. Many do little more than enter your home in the MLS, put a sign in the yard, and that's it. Some will not even show the house for you. Others charge a flat fee, plus additional a la carte fees for other services. For instance, $1,500 flat fee, plus $50 per Open House, $200 for adding to the brokerage website, etc… By the time you're done, you probably are going to pay as much as you would to a brokerage that charges on a percentage basis but includes everything in the price. I am not knocking all Flat Fee Brokers, because there are some that do a very good job. Just make sure you understand exactly what it is you are paying for.

6. ADVENTURES IN MARKETING

Every single agent that you interview, or who gives you a listing presentation, will tell you that they have the best marketing available and are heads and shoulders above their competition. While it is true that some agents go above and beyond for their clients in many ways, the marketing tends to be almost identical from one agent to another, regardless of what brokerage they are with.

I first received a real estate license well before the dawn of the internet age. Back then an MLS book would come out once per month in our market. The MLS book consisted of all the homes listed for sale. Each listing would have one black and white picture of the front of the house, along with an abbreviated description of the property, and contact information for the listing agent. When we took a new listing, we would fill out an MLS form, then it was sent into the company that published the books. There could be a turnaround time from two weeks to a month before your listing made it into a print copy of the book, and there were no digital copies. If you had a buyer looking for a home, you would have to thumb through the book to find ones that fit their criteria, and then set up a showing with the listing agent. It was quite a cumbersome process.

In those days it was much more difficult to market, as you can imagine. The agent needed to get the word out that he had a listing for sale. He or she could promote the listing to other agents in the office, put a sign out in the yard, and put an advertisement in the local newspaper. Of course, an Open House was another way to try to get people through the door. But if an agent was lazy, they would just put the listing in the MLS book, put a sign out front, and hope the home sold.

Today, it is a much different world when it comes to real estate, and especially when it comes to marketing a property for sale. Every single agent in your local real estate board has the same basic tools at their disposal, no matter which brokerage they are with. While their particular brokerage might offer a couple more bells and whistles than the one down the street, they are extremely similar. Every agent also has access to a professional photographer to take pictures of your home. If they are not willing to include professional photography as part of the listing package, I would not consider hiring them. I understand cell phones take great pictures these days, but they still are no substitute for professional photographs taken by a photographer who specializes in taking photos of homes.

Now when you begin talking to a listing agent, they will probably tell you that within a couple of hours of you signing the listing agreement, your home will be featured online, and within 24-48 hours, it will appear on well over 200 real estate related websites, including major sites like Zillow and Realtor.com. Incredible, isn't it! But guess what? They simply entered in the information and uploaded the photographs to their local MLS. Every MLS worth their salt has a paid arrangement with an online distribution system which feeds the listing to all of the websites your agent just told you about. Which means that every broker who is a member of the local board and MLS (which is practically all of them) is doing the exact same thing. What brokerage they are with has absolutely nothing to do with it. When the agent proudly proclaims this is a service their office provides, they are telling you the truth. But so are all the other agents from all the other brokerages.

Here is the unvarnished truth – almost all marketing an agent does begins and ends with inputting the listing information and photographs into the MLS! In addition, most all real estate brokerages are a part of the IDX (Internet Data Exchange), which allows them to share all their listing data on each other's websites.

> [x]For real estate agents and brokers in the US, IDX is the system that allows REALTORS® to show MLS property listings on their websites. IDX stands for "Internet Data Exchange", which sounds technical, but really it's quite simple from the agent's perspective. IDX is sometimes called Broker Reciprocity due to the fact that brokers

participate by allowing other MLS board members to display their property listings.

What this means is that every real estate agent and broker's website is allowed to share every other real estate agent's listing no matter what brokerage they happen to belong to. It is a cooperative arrangement to get a listing the most possible exposure. It is a wonderful tool and a welcome addition to marketing homes. But it is also a tool that is fully built into the system and automated. Again, your agent simply inputs the listing information and photographs into the MLS, and this process takes over from there. While you might think your agent is laboring over their computer, sending this information out to all the major real estate websites and convincing other brokers to advertise your listing, it is already in the mix from the moment they hit the submit button on their MLS input form. There is absolutely nothing wrong with this, but some less than honest agents will misrepresent it as if it is something exclusively offered by them, or something that is done by them personally and that is one of the reasons they have to charge you a higher commission.

The important thing to note is that it barely ever matters what brokerage your agent is with since they all share almost identical tools. Most potential buyers do not care which sign is in your front yard. What is important is that you get the right agent, and every brokerage has good ones, bad ones, and mediocre ones.

While most agents begin and end their marketing with inputting the listing into the MLS, there are definitely some wonderful exceptions. Some go out of their way to promote themselves and your listing on social media. Others will offer to make professional grade videos of your home. Still others have built up a huge network of other area real estate agents who they are able to contact directly and personally with information about your home in the hopes that they might have a buyer ready to act on it. Some have built up a significant email list of potential buyers and investors that they can send your home to which is a very valuable tool.

Open Houses are another way good agents market your home. These have been a source of debate among real estate agents for decades. Some say that the only reason agents want to do Open Houses is to try to get buyer leads. While Open Houses are a good source of buyer leads, they are also a great way to expose a home to the market and potentially sell it. Any agent who tells you that a house cannot be sold at an Open House does not know what they are talking about. They are either just repeating what others have said, they are really not very good at selling, or they are too lazy to take a Saturday or Sunday afternoon to try to sell your home. And yes, if you're wondering, I have sold multiple homes at Open Houses.

If you interview a real estate agent who is not willing to do Open Houses, I would start talking to other agents who will. Even if the listing agent does not want to personally do the Open House, there are plenty of eager agents in their office that would be willing to do the Open House for them. It is a great way for newer agents to get their feet wet, and while they might not have tons of experience, most have plenty of enthusiasm, which can go a long way toward getting your house sold.

You are looking for an agent that goes above and beyond the norm, and thankfully, there are quite a few of them out there. Don't be satisfied until you find one of them.

7. DOES EXPERIENCE MATTER?

When it comes to hiring a real estate agent, whether they are helping you sell a home, buy a home, or both, how much experience should you look for? We all know that everyone has to start somewhere, but do you want a complete newbie overseeing the sale and transfer of your most valuable possession, or do you trust them to have the know how to get you the best deal and financing on the buying end?

This can be a tough subject because just like in any other field there are newer people that catch on quickly and have an aptitude for this business, and there are others who have many years of experience, but they have never really been good at it. That being said, in most cases the only way

I would hire someone with less than three- or four-years' experience would be if they were working very closely with an experienced mentor. There are just too many things that can go wrong.

I realize that if you don't hire your niece Kathy, who is a very nice gal who just got her real estate license last month, you are going to have some people upset with you. But better that than you having to deal with a mistake that could literally cost you tens of thousands of dollars. Of course, everything might go fine, but chances are, she is not going to be prepared to do the best job for you, no matter how good her intentions might be. Because while a lot of the marketing looks the same and is on auto-pilot whether you have a brand new agent or one who has been doing this for decades, the agent walks a very lonely road when it comes to actually working out all the details and kinks in contracts, inspections, appraisals, and getting everything ready for Closing. There is a LOT that could go wrong, and a LOT of knowledge is necessary.

Let me list for you some rookie mistakes to give you a better idea of why I take this so seriously. I am aware that some experienced agents make these same mistakes, but there can be no doubt that they are more common with newer agents. Also, you need to be aware that I am not an attorney and I am not offering legal advice. If you have legal questions, please consult an attorney that specializes in real estate issues.

Placing the Wrong Value on a Home

I decided to list the biggest one first. When it comes to placing a value on the home you are going to sell, or on the home you are wanting to buy, you better know what you are talking about. As mentioned in an earlier chapter, none of these nuts and bolts issues are covered in studying for the real estate license. Hopefully, the agent has a good broker and/or mentor who is able to teach them how to place a value on a home, but you'd be surprised how many are out there just winging it. When I first got my license I priced the very first home I had a chance at listing at $50,000 and really thought it was a good price. The seller went with a different agent who knew much more than I did at the time and sold the home for $80,000. If he had went with me, he would have lost $30,000.

The bottom line is the seller wants to sell for as much as they possibly can, and the buyer is wanting to pay as little as possible. What really matters is what the home is worth on today's market. Good agents will do a CMA (Comparative Market Analysis) on the home that will give them a very good idea of what the home is worth. If you are selling a home, your agent should do a CMA on the home you are selling, and if you are buying a home your agent should do a CMA on the home you want to purchase. I won't go into all the details of a CMA here, but if it is done right it will compare all of the most similar homes in the closest possible vicinity that have sold in the most recent timeframe. That, along with upgrades, home value trajectories in the area, and other factors are at play.

You would be shocked at how many agents do absolutely no research in placing a value on a home. In many internet MLS programs they will have an option to click a button and have an automated CMA which will be produced in seconds. These are highly inaccurate and include homes that are simply not comparable to the target home. There is nothing wrong with using a computer program to come up with a value, but when you go the automated route, you will almost always come out with something that does not resemble what the home is really worth. The agent needs to painstakingly go through each listing and make sure it is comparable, make allowances up or down for different features, quality, upgrades, neighborhood, and other items that effect price. And even when a new agent takes all the right steps, their lack of experience will often lead them to a wrong value. I have run automated CMAs out of curiosity using different computer models and had wildly differing results on the exact same home. I've also run them and compared them to homes after they've sold just to see how far off the automated program was. One that stands out valued a home at $600,000. That home sold a few months later for $850,000. If the agent who listed that house had used the automated CMA, they could have cost the seller $250,000. That is the worst one I've seen, but it can happen. Many times it goes the other way, and the automated program over prices the home. The truth is, with a good agent who knows how to prepare a CMA, you can come up with a price that is almost exactly what the home is worth.

Missing Deadlines

Whether you are on the buying or selling side there are deadlines that are written into the contract that must be met. Let's say you are the buyer and your contract says you will have a professional inspection of the property within 14 days of contract acceptance and then will negotiate any repairs. What if your agent overlooks this detail and doesn't let you know that the inspection you have scheduled for the 15th day after contract acceptance is not only going to let the seller off the hook for any potential repairs, but now you most likely cannot get out of the contract, even if they find some major issues?

Most contracts also state what type of financing you have and what amount of Earnest Money you are putting down. They also normally state that the loan must be locked in within a certain number of days. If you are on the buying side and you don't lock the loan in within the specified period, most likely the seller can cancel your contract and accept a better offer. Your agent needs to be on top of this. Or let's say you are the seller and the deadline goes by for locking in the loan, but your agent doesn't make you aware of that. In fact, the buyer hasn't done anything with the loan at all. You get to the day before Closing only to find out that the buyer is not going to be able to buy your house. You've just wasted 30-40 days of your home not being on the market, and depending on the circumstances, might not be able to purchase the home you have a contract on.

If you look at an Offer to Purchase Contract you will see there are numerous deadlines like these that must be met. But you will find agents, generally new ones, that treat these as if they don't really matter, or don't even know that they are there.

Lack of Communication

A good agent is in constant communication with their client, lenders, contractors, and anyone else who is involved in a particular transaction. With cell phones, texting, email, and internet, there is just no excuse to not be in good communication. That doesn't mean an agent should have to take a call at 2:00 am because you're thinking you should be looking at two-story homes instead of single-story, but they should at least get back to you promptly. I cannot tell you how many deals have went awry because an agent dropped the ball on communication. Picture everyone involved with the transaction as the spokes on a wheel, and the agent being the hub at the center. That is how it works. The agent is the one person everyone involved communicates with to keep the deal moving forward. If they decide, for whatever reason, not to be the hub, everything starts to fall apart.

Fighting with other Agents

Many agents are very combative when it comes to working with agents on the other side of a negotiation. While each agent works for his or her client's best interests, they also need to work together. It is not unusual for a new agent to take things personally and lash out. For instance, let's say the home is under contract and has just had an inspection. The buyer's agent contacts the new (listing) agent and gives them a repair list that needs to be negotiated, and there are some very unreasonable repairs on the list. The buyer wants the seller to put in new carpet, paint the living room, and refinish the wood floor in the spare bedroom. These are all things that the buyer saw when viewing the house, they are cosmetic items, and there is no reason the seller should have to repair them. Rather than respond in a kind way that gets the point across that the repairs will not be done, the new agent says, "I can't believe your idiot clients expect my people to fix that stuff. It ain't gonna happen and you can all shove it." If you think that's an exaggeration of what can happen, it's not. Many agents think that getting tough with other agents is a good negotiation tool – it's not.

The end result is that everyone is tense, and what could have been a smooth deal, ends up being a very bad experience for everyone. This type of thing happens all too often with people who just find it hard to communicate in a businesslike manner.

The bottom line is that you can have both new and experienced agents who make these kinds of errors. But in my opinion, you take a greater chance with a new agent than an experienced one.

8. INTERVIEWING AGENTS

This is the way most people pick a real estate agent. They simply do a quick search online and contact the first agent that looks like they aren't a serial killer. Some go the extra mile and ask a couple of friends if they liked the agent they used, then call one of those agents. If they are selling, they have the agent come to their house, sign all the listing paperwork, and hope everything turns out okay. If they are buying, they either pick out some houses they want to see or tell the agent what type of home they are interested in and let the agent pick.

Here is what you should do. There is nothing wrong with asking your friends if they have an agent they have been happy with. If they were pleased add that person to your list. Call a couple of brokers in town and ask them to name their two best agents. If they hesitate, ask them who they would hire from their office if they were selling or buying a home. If the broker names him/herself, move on. You want to come up with a list of about 6-8 names.

Get online and search out each name. Look on Facebook, Twitter, LinkedIn, Pinterest, and any other Social Media you can think of. Check out their real estate website. If they have little to no presence online, cross them off your list. In this day and age, if they don't know how to use these resources, they are not for you. Look at their picture. Are they professional looking? While we don't want to hold their personal social media posts to a professional standard, you can probably get a feel for what they are like and how they present themselves. If they are a big turn-off, cross them off your list. Look at their reviews online and see what they say. It is not unusual for even a great agent to have a couple of less than perfect reviews, but if they have consistently bad ones, cross them off.

The goal is to get your list down to about 3-4 agents that you think you might want to work with. Now it's time to schedule interviews.

Call each agent on your list. Again, you don't want more than four. If you go through this process and none of them work out, you can start over again. But if you do what was suggested above, I am almost certain you will be able to find 1 or 2 good agents and will only have to go through this process once.

When you call each agent, let them know what you are planning to do. If you are buying, let them know that. If you are selling, tell them. If you are doing both, share that as well. Now you need to set an appointment for them to meet with you individually. Please do not set up a group interview. It will be a disaster for everyone involved. Let each agent know that you will be interviewing multiple agents and you will not be deciding until you have completed the interviews. I can guarantee you that at least one will try to get you to sign a listing or buyer's agreement before they leave, even though you've told them you are not making a decision yet. If they do, I would cross them off my list. I would suggest meeting in your home. It is also best to do this over a course of a day or two so everything is fresh in your memory. Plan for about an hour for each interview.

When they come for the interview, make note of what they bring with them. If they come empty handed and just expect you to work with them, cross them off the list. If they are that unprepared when they are interviewing to potentially make thousands of dollars, they are going to be unprepared in helping you buy or sell a house as well. If you are selling, they should give some type of listing presentation. Some do it digitally, while others do it on paper. They should include home values of listings that have sold over the last six months in your area. I would also expect them to tell me about their experience, how long they've been in the business, about their company, and other information designed to help you build confidence in their abilities.

Here is a list of solid interview questions.

You do not have to use all of these, and some might be answered prior to you getting to this list, but it is a good overview. Feel free to add your own or reword these.

1. How long have you been licensed in real estate?

2. Are you a full-time or part-time agent?

3. How many homes did you sell in the last 12 months? How many of those were listings and how many were you the buyer's agent? Have you had any listings that didn't sell? If so, why do you think they didn't sell?

4. How do you use the internet and social media to sell homes or to find homes for buyers?

5. Do you have good relationships with lenders? Which ones do you usually recommend? What are the current rates?

6. Have you lived in this area very long?

7. What sets you apart from other agents I might interview?

8. How often will you be in touch with me and what methods do you normally use? Text, E-mail, etc...

9. Have you ever received any disciplinary action by the Real Estate Board or your broker?

10. Do you or your brokerage charge any type of fees other than the commission?

The following questions are specifically for listing agents:

11. What is the best way to price our home? Do you manually put together a CMA or do you use an automated process?

12. What is your normal commission rate? How flexible are you on that?

13. What is your normal listing period? Are you willing to list for 90 days and then have a discussion with me about extending the listing if it doesn't sell in that amount of time?

14. Do you use a professional photographer? Do you use video?

15. Other than placing the information in the MLS, what types of marketing do you do?

16. How often will you do an Open House? Do you do them yourself or have another agent do them for you?

17. Do you have a large personal network of agents you can share our home with?

The following questions are specifically for buyer's agents:

18. Who finds the homes we will go see? Does the client usually send them to you, or do we give you our criteria and you look for us?

19. Is the home inventory high or low for our area?

20. What are the basic differences between Conventional, FHA, and VA loans?

21. If we find a home that we want to put an offer on, are you willing to do a CMA on it to help us know how much to offer?

22. Do you have a list of inspectors and contractors you usually recommend?

23. Do you use a Buyer's Representation Agreement? If so, do you insist on a buyer signing it in order to work with you?

As you can see, that is a pretty thorough list. If you ask all of the relevant questions, you should be pretty well informed on each agent you interview. By the time you are done, most likely one agent will stand out.

9. SIGNING PAPERWORK

It is impossible to tell you exactly what your paperwork will consist of, since each State, and even County/City might be different. But we can go over the basics. In almost every case these forms have been prewritten by attorneys and cannot be changed, other than the areas where there are blank spaces. There might also be places where additional information can be filled in. If you have any legal questions concerning any of this paperwork, please consult a real estate attorney. *I am not here to give legal advice, just practical advice.*

Paperwork when Selling

If you're selling your house there will be a Listing Packet with paperwork for you to sign. The main form you will be signing is the Listing Agreement. In most areas the most common is the [xi]*Exclusive Right to Sell* Agreement. The main things you need to be concerned about in this agreement are the commission percentage and the number of days you agree to be under the listing agreement contract.

We discussed commission percentages in detail in Chapter 5, so I won't go over that again. But you need to make sure your agent enters the agreed upon amount on the listing agreement. Some agents "forget" how much was agreed upon and end up putting a higher amount on the paperwork. Don't sign the agreement until this amount is filled in.

The length of the agreement is another negotiable item. Most agents will want you to list for six months (180 Days). I would try to negotiate this down to 90 Days, or 120 Days at most. If the home has not sold in the specified time, but you feel your agent has done a good job, you can sign an extension of the agreement. If you don't feel they have done a good job, you are free to list with a different agent. You do not want to tie your house up for 180 Days with an agent who isn't working.

Most likely you will also be filling out a *Seller's Disclosure.* On that disclosure you will need to honestly list any problems you presently have with the house, repairs you have done, age of the roof, HVAC, and more. Some are more detailed than others. Make sure you fill this out very thoroughly and honestly. It is the right thing to do, and you could be sued if you don't.

There is other paperwork you most likely will need to sign. These vary with different areas, and even with different companies. *Again, if you have any questions, consult a real estate attorney.*

Paperwork when Buying

In years past the buyer did not sign anything until it was time to make an offer to purchase. Now many buyer's agents will ask you to sign a *Buyer's Representation Agreement.* Some agents will not show you any homes unless you sign this agreement. Some will take you out once, but won't show you any more until after you sign. The reason they want you to sign is because it binds you to that particular agent and brokerage for a specified period of time, usually 180 Days. This is understandable, since they are going to spend a significant amount of time and energy trying to find you a home. For an agent one of the worst things that can happen is to show a client 30 homes, and then the client ends up buying through a different agent. It happens all the time, and the agent who did most of the work doesn't receive a dime.

And while this is true, I would be very hesitant to sign a Buyer's Representation Agreement for the following reasons:

1) You are tied to that particular agent, even if you decide you don't want to work with them any longer. While you can usually give a 10 Day Written Notice to get out of the agreement, it can be a hassle and will keep you out of the house buying market for at least 10 days.

2) Most buyer's representation agreements state that if the seller is not willing to pay a certain amount in commission, then the buyer agrees to make up the difference. This happens often with For Sale By Owners. Let's say the FSBO says they are willing to pay your agent 1.5% commission, but your *Buyer's Representation Agreement* says your agent will be paid 3% commission. Guess who has to

make up the difference? That's right, the buyer. What happens if the FSBO won't pay any commission at all, but you really want the house? Again, you will be paying the commission. So, on top of coming up with Escrow Money, Down Payment, Closing Costs, and other expenses, you now have to pay the commission as well.

My advice? Don't sign a Buyer's Representation Agreement, BUT, be loyal to your agent and only buy through them if they have been doing a good job for you.

Once you find a home you want to buy one of the most significant papers you will sign is the *Offer to Purchase*. Again, these vary from place to place, but the negotiable items are usually the purchase price, amount of escrow money, down payment, type of financing, what stays with the house, what type of inspection, if any, and date of Closing. There might be more or less depending on your area. Your agent should be able to guide you through all of this and explain it thoroughly.

You will most likely also be signing the *Seller's Disclosure*, showing that you have thoroughly read through it and understand it. There will most likely be more paperwork than this, but again, this will vary depending on location.

10. ODDS AND ENDS

In this chapter I'd like to deal briefly with several topics that should be of interest to you that do not warrant an entire chapter of their own.

For Sale By Owner

As a real estate agent I was constantly confronted with the issue of people either wanting to sell their house on their own, or someone wanting to purchase a home that someone wanted to sell without involving any real estate agents. We call those who sell their home without an agent "For Sale By Owners" or FSBO for short. The reason for this is obvious from the seller's side – they can potentially save thousands of dollars selling it on their own. From the buyer's side it doesn't make as much sense, because in most areas they do not pay a buyer's agent anything to help them find a home and work through all the nuances of the deal. In addition, most FSBOs are overpriced. For some reason many of them think their home is worth more if they don't have an agent. What they don't realize is that most buyers expect to get their home at a lower price because they realize the seller is not having to pay a commission.

The big question for sellers is – should you try to do it on your own? Consider these statistics that come from the National Association of Realtors®:

[xii]For Sale By Owner (FSBO) Statistics

FSBOs accounted for 11% of home sales in 2018. The typical FSBO home sold for $200,000 compared to $280,000 for agent-assisted home sales.

FSBO methods used to market home:
    *None: Did not actively market home: 36%
    *Yard sign: 31%
    *Open house: 24%
    *Friends, relatives, or neighbors: 21%
    *Multiple Listing Service (MLS) website: 20%

*Online classified advertisements: 13%

*Social networking websites (e.g. Facebook, Twitter, etc.): 11%

*For-sale-by-owner websites: 5%

*Direct mail (flyers, postcards, etc.): 4%

*Video: 1%

*Print newspaper advertisement: less than 1%

Most difficult tasks for FSBO sellers:

*Getting the right price: 19%

*Preparing/fixing up home for sale: 13%

*Selling within the planned length of time: 7%

*Having enough time to devote to all aspects of the sale: 5%

*Understanding and performing paperwork: 3%

In my opinion it is worth selling your home yourself if you have the time and ability to pull it off. If you don't have to sell immediately you might try for a couple of months and if you don't have any success, hire a qualified real estate agent. It is beyond the scope of this book to give you detailed instructions on how to go about doing this, but you will definitely need to contact a real estate attorney in your area and make sure you have all the right paperwork and are taking the proper steps. I would suggest calling a couple of local Title companies to see if they can help. Most big box office stores carry the basic paperwork you will need, or you might be able to just download it online, but again, verify with a real estate attorney that it is what you need before purchasing and/or using it.

If you do decide to sell yourself, get ready for an onslaught of calls and visits from real estate agents. Many agents spend the bulk of their time trying to get FSBO to list with them. There are many courses and systems available that agents purchase with scripts, boiler plate letters, and much more, teaching them how to convert you from selling your home yourself to listing it with them. Here is one example of many I could share with you – www.fsborino.com

On the other hand, if you are buying a home, I would look at everything available that is listed by a real estate agent before I would look at any FSBO. As I stated above, most are way overpriced, and often the owner has no idea what they are doing. Unless you are very familiar with the real estate process in your area and are confident you can get inspections, appraisal, repairs, etc… done correctly and on time, it is simply not worth the hassle.

Dual Agency

In States where Dual Agency is legal, the real estate agent may work on behalf of both the Seller and Buyer in the transaction. At the time of this writing Dual Agency is illegal in the following States:

Alaska

Colorado

Florida

Kansas

Maryland

Oklahoma

Oklahoma

Texas

Vermont

An example of dual agency would be the following – you have your house listed with Jane Doe of Acme Real Estate. A potential buyer contacts Jane and wants to see your house. The buyer falls in love with the house and wants to put an offer on it. Jane contacts you with the good news, but informs you, "I would like to represent both you and the buyer in this transaction and will need you to sign a form stating you are okay with that if it sounds good to you."

Up until this point, Jane has been working exclusively for you and in your best interest. If she also begins a relationship with the buyer, she also must represent their best interest as well. Can that be done? Will she be able to represent both parties in negotiations? That is where the debate comes in. Some say it is impossible for an agent to treat both parties equally.

The reality of dual agency is that the agent will have to walk the tightrope of complete neutrality, neither siding with the buyer or seller. They will not be able to share any information derived from either party. So, if the buyer tells Jane, "I am willing to go up to $250,000 on my offer" she cannot share that information with the seller. Or if the seller says, "I would take $245,000 on this house if they offered it," Jane cannot share that information with the buyer. Then of course, there are negotiations over the home inspection, potential issues with financing, and other concerns that cannot be shared.

The benefit of dual agency for the real estate agent is obvious – their brokerage will receive the entire commission. Instead of splitting a 6% commission with another brokerage, they will keep the entire thing. Instant Double Payday!! They will have to work harder, but is it worth twice as much? And do you trust the agent to stay completely neutral? In addition, you hired them to work on your behalf, and now they are no longer able to do that. Is that fair to either party?

If you tell the agent you do not want to accept dual agency, they will usually recommend a different agent from within their brokerage to the buyer or another agent they are friends with. They also will often expect that agent to pay them a referral fee for recommending them.

I personally would avoid dual agency. There is very little benefit, if any, to anyone but the real estate agent. There is a reason this is illegal is so many States.

Junk Fees

Many brokerages charge a fee in addition to the commission. They go by different names, such as ABC Fee,

Document Fee, Administrative Fee, and more. Most charge it to you whether you are a buyer or a seller. I've seen them as low as $95 and as high as $400. If you'll remember in our suggested interview questions we included:

10. Do you or your brokerage charge any type of fees other than the commission?

Sometimes this fee is charged directly by the broker and in that case the real estate agent usually doesn't receive any of this. In other cases the real estate agent is charging this fee directly and receives all of it.

I would not pay this fee. It is a "junk fee" just like the Document Fee you pay when you buy a car from a dealership. If you are a seller, you are already paying a substantial percentage of your proceeds to the brokerage that sells your house. If you are a buyer any money your agent has earned is already being paid from the seller's commission. Simply ask the agent to cross out and everyone initial any part of the contract that mentions this fee. If they aren't willing to do that, I'd find another real estate agent. There are many who do not charge this fee.

Real Estate Teams

There are many real estate agents these days that are a part of a team. There are different kinds of teams. Some might be a married couple working together, or a partnership between two or more agents with different strengths and weaknesses. Usually these types of teams share the different tasks involved in working with buyers or sellers and share equally in the expenses of doing business, as well as the profits.

The more popular team usually consists of one successful agent, known as the "rainmaker" who has other agents working for him or her as buyer's agents and listing agents. The rainmaker draws in all the leads and then disperses them to the agents on the team. Those agents then give a percentage of their split back to the rainmaker when the deal is closed. So, the rainmaker takes a portion of the team agent's commission.

It would look something like this:

Commission total:

$10,000

Agent split with brokerage: 80/20

$8,000

Rainmaker split with agent on team: 50/50

$4,000

In the above scenario both the Rainmaker and the Team Agent would receive $4,000. There are numerous ways of doing this, but the bottom line is, the Rainmaker receives a commission on every sale the team agents make. Their split from one agent to the next might differ considerably.

While I would not hesitate to hire an agent in the first scenarios (married team, partner team) that meet the criteria we have listed, I would be very hesitant to hire a team led by a rainmaker. Here are two reasons why:

1) The rainmaker team advertises the rainmaker because this agent has been highly successful. That is a good thing. Usually it is the rainmaker whose picture is on all the advertising. But guess what? The chances of you actually

having the rainmaker work with you personally is very slim. Most of them view themselves as a manager of the agents on their team, not a hands-on agent working with clients. Many clients who hire this type of team never even meet the rainmaker. It is very similar to the huge law firms that you see advertisements for on TV. The big-name lawyer is in all the commercials, but if you hire that law firm, you are going to work with one of the staff.

2) On most rainmaker teams, the buyer's and seller's agents have very little experience. That is why they joined the team. They want to work under an experienced agent who can give them leads. There is nothing wrong with that. Any real estate agent will tell you that the most difficult part of the business is getting qualified leads to work with. Many agents pay thousands and even tens of thousands of dollars every month to internet lead sources to feed them business and most of those leads are no good. So, to have leads handed to you, especially as a new agent, is worth paying the rainmaker for. Once these agents get some experience under their belt, they usually leave the rainmaker's team and work on their own because they don't want to have to keep splitting their commission

twice (once with the broker, and once with the rainmaker). It is not at all unusual for these agents to leave within a year or less.

Those are my reasons for not hiring a rain maker team. It is possible that you could find an agent on one of these teams that is experienced and is a member of the team for reasons other than I have stated above. In that case, you might consider hiring them. Just use good judgment.

Home Security

If you are selling your home and it goes on the MLS, Craigslist, or any other source of advertising, potential home buyers aren't the only ones who are going to see it. Everyone who looks at the ads will know your address, the basic layout of the house, and see your possessions in the pictures (unless the house is vacant). I don't want to alarm you too much, but you do need to be aware. From my experience I have not heard of many instances when a home was broken into due to an ad, but it can happen.

If you don't already have some type of alarm or camera system, this would be a good time to get one. You can buy a camera system that runs on your home's Wi-Fi very inexpensively and if it isn't hard wired through the house, you should be able to take it with you when you move (just make sure and note that in your listing paperwork). This way you should at least have a video record of what is taking place in your home. You will need to check the laws where you live, but in many places you are allowed to video people who are walking through your home on showings, although audio is often restricted. If you are going to do this, I would also have your real estate agent put that in their listing remarks so buyers are aware they are being filmed. That might or might not be necessary from a legal basis, but personally, I find it in bad taste not to let them know.

You will want to make sure that any loose valuables, such as jewelry is either locked up, or you take it with you. The same goes for medication. There are unscrupulous people who will visit your home and go through your medicine cabinet. Unfortunately, there are drug addicts who see your home as an easy target. If you have any firearms, make sure they are inaccessible. If nothing else, put them in the trunk of your car during showings. Be especially diligent when you host an Open House.

Home Preparation

It should go without saying, but I have shown many homes that were absolutely filthy, with clothes, garbage and general clutter everywhere. Then there have been many others that were in disrepair. For instance, it is not unusual to walk into a $500,000 home with a toilet falling through the floor due to unchecked leakage. If you are trying to sell your home, you want it to look better than it has ever looked before. If it is a $50,00 investment property, that might be an exception to the rule, but even with a home like that, you should present it as best you can. You will want to get your home ready before taking photographs, planning an Open House, or scheduling Showings.

Improve the exterior of your home to boost curb appeal:

> *Mow the lawn, trim the trees and bushes, and get rid of any plants that look sick. You can also add some colorful flowers.

*Clean your yard and get rid of anything that looks old or damaged. Fix any holes in your fence and throw away your old lawn furniture or restore it with a new coat of paint.

*Paint the outside of your home if needed. Wash the outside of the windows and paint the window trim.

*Inspect your roof, clean it, and replace a few shingles if needed. Fix any broken gutters and clean them.

*If you don't own one, rent a pressure washer. Use it to clean the outside of your home, your shed, your driveway, and the sidewalk in front of your home.

* Get a new mailbox and house number if necessary.

You'll also need to prepare the inside of your home:

*Eliminate as many items as possible to make your home look less cluttered. You could pack all the items you don't need and keep the ones you use on a daily basis in boxes that can easily be put away.

*Put away photographs, décor items, mementos, and other personal objects. Make your home look as neutral as possible so that potential buyers can visualize themselves living here.

*Clear up as much space as possible to make rooms seem larger. Put furniture into storage if needed.

*Repaint with neutral colors. If some of your rooms are painted with bright colors or if you've used a stencil when painting, apply a new coat of paint in a neutral color.

*Make your home look newer by painting windows, doors, and cabinets. Replace old outlets, light fixtures, door handles, and cabinet doors.

*Fix small problems such as leaking faucets, damaged floor tiles, or cracks in walls.

*Replace items such as rugs, curtains, or bedspreads with more neutral ones.

*Clean your entire home. Wash the walls and wax the floors. Apply new caulk where needed.

*Use a professional carpet cleaning service or rent a steam cleaner to get rid of any stains.

Buying "As-Is"

In most real estate markets, you will be given an option on the Offer to Purchase contract concerning Inspections and Repairs. With so much variation from State to State, I can't get into a detailed discussion, but I can give you a generalized summary.

While some contracts allow you several options concerning the inspection, the bottom line is, as the buyer, you are either going to get one or not. Typically, you will hire a licensed inspector who will perform an inspection on the property you are wanting to purchase. At the end of the inspection you will be given a list, usually along with photographs, of suggested repairs that need to be done to the house. You then, along with your real estate agent if you have one, will make a list of those repairs that you think the seller should be responsible for fixing. These normally do not include cosmetic items, such as paint and flooring or anything you could have easily seen while touring the house. You then can negotiate this list with the seller. If you cannot come up with an agreement, you as the buyer can normally get out of the contract and have your Earnest Money returned.

Why is it important to get an inspection? Because you could be out tens of thousands of dollars or end up with a lemon of a house if you don't. There can be all kinds of things hidden behind the walls, under the floors, on the roof, in the furnace, and a whole bunch of other places you've probably never considered. Many times, the seller is not even aware of these items that need repair, but sometimes they are and are hiding them from you. Have you priced a furnace or new HVAC system lately? What if there are major cracks in the foundation? How about a big leak in the roof covered over by paint? I could go on and on.

So, we've established the need for an inspection, which brings me to the point about buying a home "as-is." In many markets the seller can decide to list their home "as-is." This means just what it sounds like. The buyer is going to make an offer and accept the home just the way it sits. No repairs will be done. In some areas you can still do an inspection, but the repairs will not be negotiated, and the seller is not obligated to make any no matter what is found. The good news, in most cases, is that the buyer can walk if they find something in the inspection that they don't like or that is going to be too costly for them to repair, and have their Earnest Money returned.

The only time I would consider buying a home "as-is" is if it were a very low-cost investment property that I was already planning on sinking some money into. In other words, a "gut job." If I'm going to have to strip it down to bare bones anyway, I am not as worried about repairs, but the truth is, you could still run into some things you weren't planning on fixing that could get expensive.

The bottom line – unless you run across the deal of the century, I would advise you not to buy a home "as-is." And if you do run across such a deal, look a little closer.

It's probably not as great as you think it is. There could be a variety of reasons a homeowner wants to sell "as-is." They simply might not have enough money to do any repairs, or they are just the type that don't want to mess with it. Or, it could be that they know there is a lot that needs fixed and they haven't disclosed any of it. Regardless of the reason, you can find another house that doesn't have an "as-is" stipulation. Just be patient and you will find it.

CONCLUSION:

At the beginning of this book I told you that my purpose in writing was:

> ...not to steer you away from real estate agents (although in some cases they are not necessary), but to steer you away from the mediocre to bad agents, and show you how to find a good one. And if your circumstances warrant it, to encourage you to try selling your home on your own and saving a whole lot of money.

I hope that I have been able to help accomplish that for you. When taking on as daunting of a task as buying or selling a home, you need all the assistance you can get. And while professional real estate agents can be a great help, you need to make sure the one you get really is a professional!

It would be great to be able to tell you that the mediocre to bad agents are going to go away, but they've been here for decades and until the powers that be demand higher standards of excellence, you'll see them online, on billboards, and maybe even hanging up their flyer on your doorknob. Just stick to the steps you've been taught in this book and you should be fine.

In closing, let me invite you to our web page where you can ask questions, read relevant articles, get updates, and engage with others who are buying and selling homes in today's market. If we can help each other out, it will go a long way toward improving the system for everyone.

Here is the link you need: www.AgentsExposed.com

REFERENCES

i 2019 National Association of REALTORS® Profile of Home Buyers and Sellers

ii https://www.realtor.com/advice/buy/what-is-a-realtor/

iii https://www.realtor.com/advice/buy/should-i-become-a-realtor/

iv https://www.nar.realtor/education/designations-and-certifications

v https://theclose.com/real-estate-designations/

vi Real Estate Agent Facebook post.

vii https://thevaloan.org/index

viii https://thevaloan.org/certified-agent/JohnDoe

ix Real Estate Agent Facebook post.

x https://www.whatisidx.com/

xi https://www.nar.realtor/handbook-on-multiple-listing-policy/section-3-definitions-of-various-types-of-listing-agreements

xii https://www.nar.realtor/research-and-statistics/quick-real-estate-statistics